BODY WAS

ISBN: 978-1-933959-51-1
Cover artwork © Alison Rossiter, *Density 1947*, 2020
Courtesy Yossi Milo Gallery, New York
Six Gelatin Silver Prints
Framed: 15 5/16" x 17 7/16" (39 x 44.5 cm)
Design and typesetting by Mark Addison Smith

Litmus Press is a program of Ether Sea Projects, Inc., a 501(c)(3) non-profit
literature and arts organization.

Litmus Press publications are made possible by the New York State Council
on the Arts with support from Governor Kathy Hochul and the New York
State Legislature. Additional support for Litmus Press comes from the Leslie
Scalapino-O Books Fund, The Post-Apollo Press, and individual members
and donors. All contributions are fully tax-deductible.

State of the Arts

NYSCA

Litmus Press
925 Bergen Street #405
Brooklyn, New York 11238
litmuspress.org

Small Press Distribution
1341 Seventh Street
Berkeley, California 94710
spdbooks.org

Cataloging-in-publication data is available from the Library of Congress.

Printed in Canada

BODY WAS

Isabelle Garron
translated by Eléna Rivera

Suites & their variations
(2006–2009)

I can imagine nothing beyond the circle cast by my body. My body goes before me, like a lantern down a dark lane, bringing one thing after another out of darkness into a ring of light. I dazzle you; I make you believe that this is all.

—Virginia Woolf, *The Waves*

Suite   1

hello   .yes   .no but
my father died this morning
I have to go to Brittany
for that yes

I won't be able to stop by   hmm
I'll meet you at the station
hmm   .have to change the time of the ticket
to quarter after yes that's doable   .okay

so in an hour then
I'll come directly
we'll meet there?
at the front   .okay

. it's early   .so many to write about
and the train stops

. on a journey   .like in the first pages of a book
someone recognizes themselves

. the train is packed and I look at you
sitting on a folding chair

I don't have words
but your gestures
abound

amid the ads
demands
doors

chasms at each sta
tion the voice—
consistent

also in the announcement
made about a delay
for

. train ahead

I look at you   .you
without staring
with

nevertheless the same
impulse as yesterday
to embrace you

while underground
the train and time
tailed obliquely

on the train and wind
the line on
which

I look at you passing
by for a long
time

an air of a whistler or
magician
or

a bit mocking per
haps between
your teeth.

. before this] it had been necessary to go back to the top alone
owing to the result of an oversight   .driving
ahead of schedule —against

our will .leaving you further down —standing amidst a
landslide .the shapes rare and everywhere
this setting sun

. this] my rage colored by this laughter of yours behind my back
that I lived .harsh—moving away

under the heat—infinite: to say the feeling-frames be
cause now to embrace you or nothing .or inscribes

the body   suffers or fatigue flips it
lets it out in one cry

sweaty toward the peak then
the cry came as if

torn out

torn out in advance
it had to do wi

th experiencing

radiance—going
back up much

later   .this radiance

that   .I would gi
-ve myself / -it?

night fallen?

the mossy night
it   .made

a necklace

then a shadow
on bodies

bore

ours in count
er

form naked

in the full
moo

n black

diffuse
tone

beneath

its design
raw milk

or otherwise

formulated tint
ed white

smashed

. higher up] signage blurred and panorama
on a city   .sky cleared oh!

this impossible good .seeing each other again
us .running beside the bay

because along the length of it I loved you yes .in
the life of the imagination—what was it?

same as   the game of the masterpiece cut
into a puzzle a piece would be missing

. really] was I alive those radiant days   knowing that
all would be contradicted that year :your body our

room those few days   the incredible rustling
outside and   the smell of mild weather

like the sea in front that breaks   I stare at it
waiting for you   eyes thick   because

in a little less than an hour   I know you're going to appear
behind my back by the front door

. it (the life imagined) between two volumes
composed of suitcases .of costs .of letters

and a few exercises—physical let's say
overlooking the city .the wave .the bay

illuminated   .and like a turn of a pedal
would chant the alphabet: to translate

the love I bore you   .in the momentum
blue trails of a form   .she, unchanged

to translate the contours of a blue form   yes
would've been in the past   the object

of a poem

to see what in the past would have been needed
to write in the same manner as

the ascent

useless at the top if only for one's own
purpose .attachment without rank

the logic

that it held   .beauty in the mirror of summer
glaciers .the bay .the wave in

electricity

—previously: meaning everything was ahead
equal   .wide open   :from the dry cleaner's
to the croissants picked up

from across the street on the return

their half mouth moon form partly given
without forgetting the receptionists
on the phone *in the large glass*

electricity in the passage mid
foreclosed on hair

between the sky's

pulleys steel gray
blue beacon

in summer

at the same time rain fell
magic beneath our feet
mist before torrents

that it dug such a
riverbed of our

steps

swamped accidentally
one day undone

under a form a

discharged patch of gold
that's how it was
that day

our electricity

now]   what has to be added is: this palpable body
makes it equal   to see it still   .and that

to slow rhythms of seaweed trampled
by you   slender as if cut

by the horizon   .on coils
of troubled color

in the freshness of your advance .and
of this river getting out of the bath

moreover partial as well as an early riser you   in these hours describe
your loss barely read digitally

a cessation? no   its lyricism

hence the train grooves that unfolded
reminding us of those in a painting

end of century much talked about

in the course of discussions a series of
clichés   from this terrace

in the red sunset .set

The moon this way always a given it had been necessary to listen and
     keep watch
. later—to be specific the smile that you gave me then
that photograph resurfaced

on my hand

prophetic the piles where flesh darkens
free of distance or memory
or distortion or

ties

she facing sea front
and you physically
my alias

lumbering gait in
a peacoat on
the border

head also fastens the
ensemble in
terior

ly

you looking exactly as if the fact of suffering
of this particular body on that steep slope
—in staccato rhythms

that stretches out with great spee
d of the one dead   .evening

the prediction that will arrive
and my lifeboat
inevitably

my lifeboat your edge and our waking
in our overnight stay already over

. remember also the tomb of three women
that had held this territory

where I set foot four days and five
nights prior to another summer

then later .faster still   .a morning of shopping
spurred on at the end of autumn

then later in one snap

fixed like the wind   my knee to the ground   its stopping point
this new space was as if opened

—followed by my lameness

then on the heels of this scene to meet again cry
out together .together—let's sing! dance!

make a fire   .fire &hell with the miracle!

to hell with the miracle   please—let's sing   on the return
with irony .or wounded—on the road   .bench
after bench .crossing   in the crosswalk

smelling the rotisserie on the way
to the butchers to hell
with the miracle!

me sweating   .same as that time of which I
speak   I couldn't   move forward
only a body

one body after another
un fou] who once in a
while grumbled

in open air—and in a zone
too exposed
also

I'd then pass right in front of the lunatic's threshold
exhibited on a hospital wall
lacerated by words

likewise I read on the ground every day
the marvelous *ancien*
lit de bras mort

you seem elsewhere you keep walking
on this buried stream

we are in September and from here
at the end of every idyll

there's always only one step
a magpie .in ochre tones

a need to scream too
into the landscape

one step then another were made therefor   .to the fire
all! to the left! when our

wishes were formed   .laces tied
at the risk of glimpsing

the form of a poem in the empty chatter
about you in my ear   .at the time

of sudden sunset   this one made law   .we
changed the register: the real

.had probably known
or thought I knew

deposited at the edge of
some summit

the d of the dead to hell
with the miracle

without partition or
voice or day

or little fairy
or anything

then you came a bit Hopi .moon in-between
and naked girl in your tired ritual
you made this sign

by discreet a
lliance   .oh!

how I
had
to fi
nd

you!

oh! sign for person and its definition—while
tornadoes kept you
indifferent .while

you chanted to the dial
a text of secrets—the
doll   she too

came—shifting the forms
the rags .the
screens

.China

its melody drawn   .the red line
peddled .seems to come

I have to write it

from other colors and
views of rivers

at the heart of the motif

all large .boats
loaded with

trade

long suffering
and songs in

common

thus descending the Niger
primary moods
were those

of a body-poem

Variation   1

you enter the room   .laundry scattered
spread out for freshness   pieces
dry

on the ledge   .it's the first time

clay. a mass of Chamotte clay on the school desk
in order to determine its use

with little invention from you .but
here I no longer see

the hands advance   .in preparation
—appears   the still life

the body born   accruing .the
it of fate

the form slides lemon against base
fear of the rest fixes .pinched
between wheel and dish

silhouettes dance amid the old rags
dirty basin water where the fiction
goes .where the form of clay
floats against walls

in the mould the acidity of citrus

vibrant peace came from elsewhere in the disorder spread
by strokes   .paintbrushes   .ribbons
tissue-papers

or other bladed tools

a beam sometimes reached the woman
that here still breathes
without her jewels

[irruption of the reaper: a man that day
enters demands reparations for the
work of his mother   he

tells how

the wings of the butterfly broke how
it's a memory she likes to see
on the wall   .how she holds
on to it a lot how she

doesn't have the strength ...]

irruption reaps: this way all can end on the shoreline. evening .or
yesterday . in order to repeat which state the offer the rainbow

was: in permanence mine by   your smile

above   .monochrome and without voice   where the range
rang faaaaaa   .fa   .then a hundred times from one

extremity of the creek to the next

I was reunited with you   . a blue on the shore where the bodies were
and already we knew it   . similarly the offering

the smell of aromatics on the lintel

similarly the mirroring of water that day   .the narration
emerging from what was facilitated by the season
and falling asleep between two plunges

reformulating tubes pools of light as much
as going through the *Penetrable*
in the labyrinth

a day in the past in which to see again moves with songs
in the color   . umpteenth   . bodies
& our flames

Now. —it's henceforth winter! the crowd presses onto steps
and the cold outside imposes on each step a measure

it's about targeting the arch   .a terrain riddled with arrows
spilling over in the question

stumbling in the face of the absent body—only a child remains
at the center of the composition   that would here spell out

her name perhaps—or that of each woman in this dreamed place
that often runs along the sea summer evenings

]mentioning a day of filming by a night of vertigo
a gypsy child   .wasn't love however

the treatment came to the eyes
your body erect—advancing

lit by the background

special effects excelled on the film set
accordingly radiant—her majesty
passed over the end of the story
a man at a piano

did the rest

a popular song for the credits was
also supposed to give us back
somewhat to our
selves that day

at least

therefore we stopped fleeing at every sunset
my little girl sleeps and we will go forward
taste the bent ridge in the fresh wind
in the pear tree a mixed odor

of resurgence

therefore I will not be the one   .I'll forget your separations
reside elsewhere. far from you   if   .if   .as long as
your comedies carry the troubling
face of a shadow on stone

in summer

elsewhere .at the threshold of gods .in another life where there was life
the perimeter receded and I cry. where
the birch's white bark folds
the farce holds .basket of
pickings in hand   al

ways I was

Suite   2

[highlights from notes: at the stop it's headlines
that comment on the election

it's autumn leaving the banks bridges
fountains   .you are no longer

in my life nor me in mine
—on quays .couples

form by dancing human
rounds .a tango circle

impossible to burst]

. later   while you look at an installation
the years behind you   .rags
lie there and here piles

under which disappeared bodies live
against other cuts of material
—at times textual

. we grew up with a view
of the whole and I'll put
these words down on
the tomb tomorrow

this hole dug for you
hastily in the earth
end of July

and it's ye
llowed tr
ees

[the pleasure of notes reread to rekindle
a fire: I like to say that I like to
decipher you as much at thirty

as at forty

—outside day enters
teeth grille gate
of signs and

The Foundation

under the sun .for the one
decor   .heat and
edits otherwise

in the air

a green and yellow song
on a blue background
—its stones

of harmony

.edits that naturally capsize
our song-order amid the
pines a single summer
rose up a single .a

parliament

on the terrace a *Steinway* ousted the scrawny
you play anything in the orange light
the certitude of a link with beauty
pervades the night to live
each tree each
form   .we

an actor

The return here a mess] to celebrate the image
of the person that goes toward the choir
accumulated in this palace
by the staircase 1900

that woman has the body of someone
that describes a kind of autopsy
the work of an elegant
shadow under
the skylight

to experience it in front
she moved the idea
of the same
mot
if

end of easy charm also noted] we must take back a body
from among visitors that advance with practice

—along with in the alleys a dissolved form of horror
She'll be the one to fix here the transparent mobile

explosive flow of crowds rounded up

essentially to write the rite of silence stripes   .fanfare in the night
here   the flowers   .the flare-ups considering   the cracks
elevation of structures of the heart   .mechanical.

his cross-fades   yes   so far   the following one   .yes
—explosive flow of crowds rounded up

later there will remain to translate the   nostalgia of notebooks

forms—of those who travel in me caved in .vanished from flat eras

previously recognized with broad strokes in certain masks

here] it's otherwise said no mountains
to paint   .to write no truth then
just all poem—arm-wrestling

with nothing

either the equation the economy
a crash insanely
accepted

and the earth

that bends here
latent and

therefore in the room a draft oscillates
awning lowered .a friend will pass

at the moment only heat   surfaces
on the ceiling our love hovers

one distinguishes quite far the whirring o
f a tractor echoes of the chicken coop

and in the vicinity a guy who practices
the trumpet outside

in the air there are gods
there is your hand
the irony

bodies the refrain
of the dance
striations

the blinds in
a dream on
your arm

and my passion would be your pitfall
maybe an open book
at the wrong page

.no stories that is   it's more of an outdoor exhibition
or routes guided by these foreign voices that raise
themselves in confession of love and something
else—the particular form

:there must be a "what"
I mean   is there gonna be a fight?

because ring or bubble
here you come
little muse

daring to put into
music some
one

at the end of a quay
where the green
flame like

that night the nocturne
of my dance
blown

you drum amulet messenger
of the voyage

in which we hear the fairy
swim in acid winds

those originating in
antique parts

murmuring between
fig leaves

this reply and
its enigma:

extend the core

because little muse one must remind the one
who has no ear silence broke ground
in the bottom of the pit

that day where you
decided me

and facing this body that finally shares its language
between the cotton and the gauze
the sheet and the square

this language to draw it give
it   the letters of a
first name

in   shaping its form

because it's really equal now facing the fort .to describe openly
marked with your cry the colorful flags of schooners
where I first saw you (two times)

—to subscribe to it despite my overly
sentimental stupor

—a life to care for it

these colorful flags of schooners where I saw you in the first place
without combinatorial nor calculation of pushing

only the idiom came to be reversed
and I improvise a song

I don't know how to play

in the blue   .firm   .infamous   —breaking
the matrix I repair it

my day your night   no night no day
if not perfect suspension

clownish color of a yellow bouquet
your hair attached

or body saying I trace it without fading .here. the possible
formulation   .square   .between silks

finally in the lights under the leaves the figurines
the paragraphs   the dolls of an artist

the grimaces of an actress   .her beauty mark
in the corner of the eye   —action!

! bah otherwise living
ranks us this way

people chanced upon

figures of passage
they walk

without myth

alight under
lean-tos

on empty chairs

under the awnings the railway platforms
the distracted paradise then
the straight lines

spoilt

but see for you I preferred to sit and contemplate updates
those theater dolls dressed for rituals
decorated in the clarity

to teach your pairs dancing
also laws between games
the toss of the jacks

that one has to catch from
one hand to another
—from one hand

the other and its pattern
in the air

before landing
retook the

jack fist closed
on the clay

court of the
players

Variation   **2**

[to find among the notes: it was long ago
that she stopped using
the farmhouse
for support

or the standing stones
for an inventory
structure or

the idioms
for small
toy

—nevertheless the opacity of the discourse continued on the side, hence
    the foreign language:
J'aime une chose comme 99: le concept d'identité est attaché à l'objet.

. therefore showcasing the morbid art of obscure lecturers one morning
    who'd come as
a delegation to try out certain rapprochements between actors of the
    public sphere

jubilant excesses. we believed in spring
but again   it's feared
that low temperatures
will return   this way

by a few degrees I realize

and we fix seasonal norms
the places you frequent
these public garden

beehives in winter.

in the news a man is dead pushed
under a train   building in front
moves us

into the light

lighting: see myself meet you again for a drink: I move
quickly to the rhythm of invented processions

if outside we hear some claim others
distinctly cry their slogans

further off at the end of the principle track
emerges the silence of the train

your arial patrols soon
for a final

calm found however outside these principle arteries
where processions advance you rethink of works
composed with their limbs
reversed

the precious waiting that of silk caressed
by silk .between us signs of types
of lingerie minuscule articles
of clothing

there. child   . you evoke the challenge of a text
in the confines of an island .here the original

imprint it's contours translated
in the snow

the fatigue of the image .of a woman
her condition .and stomach

the jolt .and
sputum

read recorded on countless occasions
I will never tell
I will write

under night the wait cracked
by a voice in the street
down below

clouds in the valley
fear too of the
return of cold

therefore   in the sun's mystifications what wonders didn't arrive
on the other side of all colors after the pale ones

of winter

I held on to the crate of apricots the newspaper from the night
before with the idea of filming the static

reading

the drop of sugar under the title .that sweats .sticks
and that afterwards comes to die out

in the fire .this orange nature

our love and its folds .on the balcony
against your thigh the suave aroma

of country alcohol

then your warm voice at the end of my
hand—a few stories to read

a round that is played

under the vines rustling—an instant
like our lives or else the fall

of ripe grapes

water that flows tonight in the furrows
the storm lingers the music also

I walked yesterday on broken glass

and today walk around
feet bandaged

. will open one's heart] in a classic portrait
your warholian face seen
duplicated

our stein-like strategies

.all the petals become roses
spill over sad sights or
the way lighting

litters the ground

.in the last part finally an annunciation to the program
on the lawn a child does a cartwheel
repeats the gesture in her stride

as a reminder

unfolds the memory of a Manet painting—that gate
painted between two worlds .then note seeing
myself write very legibly this time: extending

the verse

Suite

3

acts of centralized
hacking   lead
to the spread

how   to recover the original transaction
the fullness of knowledge

anteriority by means of studies
remains meanwhile a marker

here we are at the heart of a fragmented network
the object manually forced finds a body
amid locks the uncertain data

long before]. night in Sens on the first floor
then breakfast will follow
with one-quarter drop
shadow carried   .the
sign increasing in
your eyes

my naked delight
since yesterday
.the beauty

the walk the abbey the ebb of words
before a wave of ashes in a
cup   . same game

free

at the café . our maps   .where
to proceed? you know?
you are handsome

let's say special

for me you brea
the and on
the table

this box

of sweets offered
(customary) for
the happy

celebrations

that night in Sens had therefore read your hand
pianoforte whereby the second
song opened by

miracle .unbeknownst volume
discordant steps of
those

that didn't know *jamais*
is to say—that
I loved you

yesterday

already   .promise topography as many words where
as   I see adorned on the way back
the graphic development
of crows in season

above the plowed fields . their key
in fa on our crossings in fact

we claimed adventure at
the wheel at the stop—
similarly the music
of that small
change at
the toll
gate

which must
be ful
filled
chim
ed

brows still beating with those memorable blues
in the territory crossed those
memorable blues

of the day after in the dappled
countryside   .its opera
announced

that of a residence perched on
a three-quarter moon in the
pine forest far away .to say
everything and not

to say it once again nevertheless
in the smell of the trees
exposed to forms
end of august a
net of oil to
the collar

I was reliving there . silent admission
with one look lightning
signed by a bridge
or leaning
formerly
I hesi
tated

développé penché parallèle or
barre fixed on this balcony
all night where your body
won't have *jamais*
turned the key

the key of the unique
hand .didn't know
that night

rubbing the back of
the loved one
like on
ly

a love
of lov
e

d
o
e
s

but the night in Sens came   causing a barrier
fleeing the north   .towards the south
it was   decidedly   the
umpteenth exile

the map on the bridge the photo shoot
and by a signpost   .pointed to
sharing waters

in the lowest country .our joys painted with your visits
oh! my friends your warmth out of place
I keep a wrecked heart and this
bad taste today

inscribed by these bursts thus in the air of
the shadow   the sun of high seas
fixed its season carried in
its clouds of dust

stillbirths

strong and delightful this sun .a third round on the low wall
do you remember friends .you in your car .a
manuscript under each wheel and

a trunk full of suitcases

yet that night   at the restaurant on the square being
together at ease. the valley in front the colored
bulbs marking the exciting start

the jokes .the fragrance of thyme

at this game prolonged looks fused, forming such airs
this night   that one noticed it sometimes
in compelling company

we are young people .you beautiful ladies
odious princes charming

airs that are tied at the necks of elegant women
touching of your nape   I read
a more beautiful song

they iridescent

and you my friends
your gentleness
majestic

black dream: and if she had to break it off
I would let her do so

up to the day where we'd know how to
sleep in front of her

without her seeing me therefore
collapse in air

green shadow of the cypress the one
where weary of my night intersects

annulled ignoring it without her
who measures the flux of
signs that confused
the overflow on
the edge
of the li
ne

annulled refuses to sign
documents registers
and ornaments
sewn with
gold &
silv
er

Variation   3

[return] if the little horses of the Luxembourg
re-enter at night by the end of the street

we watch the hitting of their hooves
you open large eyes alive among automatons

note: what I lost will not
have space hereafter
only in reverse

where the lullabies in our
contrary paths
cross with

the profession the logic
wrinkled by a bitter
collective

.what pulp novel would really
have predicted the scene
with the key

the notebook   .the rendez
-vous missing the measure
suddenly

and that this body frozen by
this fear of everything
of a whole empty
story .except

in

departure   .during freefall
edge breaking off . less
telling than
sonic

who?

exhumation   .portrait   . litany recited
pink buttons, white flowers
then blackberries

who?

Who works with consequence said the shaman

the happy path of unnecessary gestures

composes music and traces forms of beauty

those who tame the angry spirits

for centuries of legends the prince's second

therefore I see you again with diligence describe points of approach
the passage of a great period .green   .reserved to insects
overtaking me nonstop in front of the described cliffs
where in the past I read this tale written by me
translated by others

words for ankles before
finishing touches
the rigor of
the plane

—translate I said, as if seeing it arrive and even feeling
it between my legs hallowed out
pushing the unexpected

one of those chiaroscuro that only a candle has—like
in the song I tell you—: "qu'à la bougie"
others painted well before

you were   but

we arrive   .it is night   .you will be born this morning

Suite   **4**

return]   .last bath of the season
first steps on this earth

new in the labyrinths
their skin is

brown

girls from the port will often go
they already possess eyes
blacker

than the olive on the tree the
sea urchin at the bottom
of the pail

our skins are close to those
of waitresses their

spouses

in the kitchen, in a boat
at the counter of

cabins

a place from where you
didn't write

me

in light of this prolonged day
something distinctive
certain and unclassifiable
finally takes place such that
the banks of the voyage
also move closer
to the end of the voyage
that the time is
short the one which
anticipated the oracle
a world that
shelters us
and what joy lies in
wait for us .if possible
in broad daylight.

London: an afternoon: splash
of color on the wall to the right
in the large room a

violet suture like velvet

on the same surface flowers printed in
orange and green tones   storm blue
surrounded by a clear sky

I fall you hold me

Upper part of the composition
will suffice to point out in
due course that a
green line

dominates .to recognize the piece
read why   land
crossed here
inverts

the leaning tower
my ship

your hand wound
ed in bramble
I fall

you hold me b
—ack

it's a movement described
everywhere

notes .palpated. clear
traces   .a readable
text . bare
ly

basically the sam
e as ten years
ago

angle of the wall   again
wide format to the left
clear rings
also form

aureoles

might as well point out that for him it began like this
:technical experiments
a painting factory

the desire to abstract
oneself

then there was the one that wrote on snow
then death then false
improvisations

an iron figurine .a carbon
print a   kind
of rupture

from elegance in the canvas
finally you   .on
the telephone

in order to divide the framework admit replaying
it in the last gallery by the fissure
on green background

these acidic colors the raw performance
of his murdering gesture

that makes me think of   .my love
the day of your divorce

outside] we walked by day with   the idea
of seeing the elephant seals
at the end of the

pier

a painting by Aurélie Nemours
on the liquid surface .thus
moves at the slow pace

of a freighter

.because I carry henceforward
a naked belly

in the unwritten
story so

in front of blue wildlife
cairns

tradeswomen crowds
a little sad

to look at together
it's nice out

comes the idea of verbalizing here open sky
:I'm waiting for a being
and at the bus stop
a bus

you smile at me a slanted smile
and the universe is said
everywhere   .I had
their age
before

we have on the
other hand
destroyed

together our first
correspon
dence

.starlit pass that resides there
pollutes. —to which
nothing resists
doesn't cross
the blade

but you are the charm
that you gave
me

I like it also when
you take my
picture

color or bl
ack and
white

the impediments of the world
press up close and turn
away arrive

finally / the breach exists
and between all
follow

the way of hands

.because from women to men I say
preferring to read a resumed
cycle   .one ap
erture . this

dream such

that in the cleavage of
Romanian snow
I saw him

write

under traces covered
too quickly the
passage of
Paul C

elan

he had fallen more than a meter
that night and the old women
had already for some time
been clearing away
the threshold
of churches

the one's with awnings more slowly while
men with a shovel and
gloves scraped in the
same cold marks
of time chased

stray dogs
pissing in
alleys

melting the white
sketch of a

road in the
city and
wind

a small bundle of young firewood
put in front of the door
of holy sites

to remove snow from the soles
of your muddy
shoes

I remember this consistent
gesture of poor
people

consistent   .quotidian   .a precise
gesture with balanced rhythm

a rhythm which
fingers frozen
I noted

I wrote against you jumbled
charms   .some

cravings

for fire for soup for
dried fruit and for

spells

as if the tale had no way out actually
except perhaps the
infinite fall

of these white yellowed pieces
under lampposts

our nights in Bucharest our nights
in the whole world

what night takes

what I shudder to read
in the night said

the night that ignores the walker ignores
us . my night

in the mountains   the night
where I lost you where

hours of our day and of
night .our finest hours

where I prayed for you to
stay to want my

laughter endlessly
by your side

night in a city where
I sleep alone

for the last time I write
that I sleep alone

ending dark blacks

images of me that you others
have selected to
take part in my

face

you you carry it in trust
to dare to write it so
dearly I cherish you

at present

Variation   4

[later]

lamb chops
cook in the
hearth

we talk in front of
the fire evening
extended

by speech while
the text
grows

with a taste of chestnuts
that of clover with
modern sound of

a crackling   .night
lightens with the
appearance

of the moon   legs
crossed back
curved the

contentment of your
dog whom
I keep

an image of
an agile
mien

yes

our shadow part subsists
:what your cry takes

in my desire

the end of what can possibly
be said at the sign of

longing

to postpone the fatality
of the dream

reread with open eyes

about the hazards
of night

words are our inventory
inhabit cooked fennel
the embers soon

ready

we were there we are no longer
there   .underline the initials
the body in front

that's stretched with each step
recognized in the magic
flux

of our own screen
our absent
pledge

there] we drink the milk then
introduce mouth

to mouth

the fruit of harvesting
there wind makes

a poem still

in times rescued from your separations
from the rift rises up
a fixed response

of a joy depleted by accretion
and facing narrations

therefore   .those who filled us hit the road
the ones that together we decided
to borrow   after them

the body cried out

between us .this anchored risk
to believe in it again to lo
ose it again   .too

bad

Suite

5

advertisements parade at one end of the road   as
        you drive
we're on the outskirts of American cities
but not exclusively

it's here there that I'm circling that there's the word
        "mot" in *Motel*
but also a brief excerpt of hell   .unless
this game falls short

of that truncated feminine   being part of the entire
        woman
that each wants to be for you: hey! I sense you
smile listening to me from the side

saying that

the little girl sleeps and we only have eyes for her
an instant   I want a cigarette I'm 30 years old
if I want   .your frown lines my love

in the rear-view mirror

hey! no melody from the dial only precious air
in time a tractor turns and the last passer-
by takes the whole parade slowly

through the fields

[well after]

your birth the very place
if this is

the passage exists and
you look at me

hand me some water
for the night

we wait for the day
that will expel
the body

we are here and
impoverished

this is the night of the
fourteenth arrondis
(-sement) before

day .your day .first

by a scarce window where I
gaze at interns electricity
all the dances

monochrome view

nothing is equal yet to the fixedness
of this night   the
calm   .the
rounds

unique all have been told unique
daylight on your forehead
which protrudes

dazzles me already

your whole body in the journey
your tribe assembled
will see to it

air passes. the harmonica .up ahead
in front the road for
the inner

vocabulary

I don't sit down—don't
walk   .I
look

before it .behind

us look at it
what it does
.there

she who sees in us harmonica
guitar hat &
cardigan

boot heels of
our love of
roads

she who will be reflected in the windows
of the sleeper-car in the song
where our glued faces

smile already ready

to go back with her
again this
time

there

but the door opens .the machine underscores that a body
comes   .that our bodies were   .that all
bodies composed

music one day

one day a body came from the spinning of rooms
of women in childbirth / beacons for
a poem

that writes itself there in the thrust

in the vertigo of the semaphore
where the air breaks
I unburden myself

you know

I would also have caressed therefor
the coarse folded
sheets of

public rooms .naked

this room your very first room
I give it to you you
give it back

hold back what of this trade
this nether world?   now
you come

into it

Variation   5

in an inverted prologue I removed the weeds
on the tomb before which you stood
straight staring at a building

the softness of the bond in front of the earth
and the crunch of the gravel
as sole chime   you

handed me some bread   facing the empty
tennis court on   .the village square
this remains an instant

a taste of cherry   in July   therefore the
fact that I didn't think of your
face   that it's here

beating by the fire   .burning even
at the time of the luncheon on th
e grass called bocages

later in front of the firn in front of the absence
of doubt and the path browning
I push away again

our vertigo

what's more natural about what was
won from the rest of the word
from which we will be quits

slow image] a man looks
at a garden down
below

a woman prunes
rose bushes
there are

blue flowers
on the tomb
stars

the green circus
in the order of
childhoods

raised on stone
hammered
dark iron

and white
furs
too

a two-wheeler passes a
second on the road
below goes off
then two

slightly stout young girls
before the strange
song of two birds
a laborer

passes youthful love
passes a view on
the world a being
in season

we are in July I
am in your life
the road isn't
straight

you say gentle words

I was occasionally a baroque singer in D.A.'s
blueprint   him his voice and   us
backpack on the waters

a whale in
a dream

very often a hamper in hand
of fine oysters
for a treat

a refrain for
oboe

big starry night okay! I wait for you
at the edge of the pier with this
falling sensation

oh! my love that suffering is
best when time comes
there to slip

we could have become before
their Argentinian faces for
I was a singer

and you knew it I think the odd
day of the opening
games

the stomach rounder she right here
beating to what was eternal
was first and poem

later .or nothing
—equally

you are my novel I'm
not inventing this
other than

to write you
off topic
a fax
lik
e

to an ex
voto

.and now—someone breathe in this cradle
that is positioned at my side
you are cold still

from a nearby chill   .identical to the
one experienced on the peaks
where our sealed embrace

opened our hearts *first lady*

today dissolved with the ends of
passages   .collars I liked
your solitude then

and your hat

what stones said on the ascension
our steps the turn your corkscrew
laughter

this fault in the rock

flight of a raptor your hand
there sweat traces
trails

law of cairns

as well as the voice of other people
on that climb the oldest
bolstered by his sons

relived the ascension

he knows it's the last his procession
reminds me of being on a road
when lowlands continue

seen from above this lake
took the form
of a heart

dark green mass it became
in the movement of light
a crown of flowers

it carries a dawn. the lake that at this hour
in side your arms and of my life

or bitterness

of a fresh charm in charge
breath and us .watchers

of a year

to year tread   earth
as well   .as storm

rolling above

above the wires
and our mad
laughter

like an abstract

fear   .of lighting that
would come like day
crashing down

when suddenly who?

who rushes down   .there where writing alongside then   .a child
who sleeps arms crossed facing us
she   .from us   otherwise dead

tilting in front of those that were   .riders
on the climb—these mountaineers
prophets at the beginning of a

poem

Suite   6

blue pot at *that* angle completes the painting

man bare-chested facing the objects
that place in the dark

crushes him   .from which he seems reborn

no possibility of severing or detaching oneself
that the contradiction carries the eye
toward the subject its deliberation

that moves off-camera   the other
practical dimension continues
to gyrate   .and to rupture

all perspectives of the studio

Niamey   .euphoric   —euphoric in a big hat
began again   upward

poetic documentary   at the half-day point
women in her group   .end of the screening

Oh evenings en plein air!

.and a spell cast—the covered angle of motion
emerges from this whitish gray a body

a form with the slowness of waters.

pale grid   .smoother upward   .sometimes weft of said
signs notwithstanding .and her fluid speech on
this love then and she'd be its

amber or the color   the inverted flesh of the mango
facing our days those that are also called blood
oh! fluid course of our debates

oh! decision makers! ancient world of that bunch—read
the word capsizing   .at each of your steps

:"that the law be told"

the law of distribution   :physics and its duration
—bread   .their effigies   .our ordinates

the port of regalia

or that which flights   figured   sometimes on the banks
bridges our beings   .notwithstanding

. evening   false :onomatopoeias and clouds be
the wind   likewise the veranda
this leather shoelace
that I carry to
your arm

.sssshhh   murmurs the words of the blown earth
gold in its pungent air and here it is that they
distinguish themselves soloists in our eyes

invaded this way orders made this way
the demarcation   .the quality of
choices

what risks neglected nonetheless
and fumes there .below .but

our exclamations burst

then this sac skin (which at 4 o'clock
you acquire) or else

an atmosphere of thunder

circulated inside .loss too .in dreams
smelling the odor of firewood

and see again these onlookers

opaque in the storefront decor
such that they marched

in memory along streets

motorized movement where living beats beating
from the beginning—and what doesn't sing
here. doesn't hear   no better

answer to base formulations
of the question originally
raised

but the enmeshment of lost souls
had the savor of vows
offered to the gods

in a night of faith
so part of it

we   . far from precipices   .far and equal to diametrically opposed
fixed orders   of said latent traps

and so I will have reread the rule   that shines and beats
at the end of voyages finished preferably

on banks   .where one observes the flight of birds
breaking into a dive with crazy speed of lords of old

to the man standing .and to the tall man?
he asks with his skin his teeth

the tall man my love is your allure
in the chanson this time   .

the chanson so aptly recalls my own the curves of statues
and when the black bird whistles

palms stir the thick air while profiles seen
from here bathe on the river

immobile you are .and he's tall too
if I sing or dance or draw

on the horizontal frame

where madrigals are composed of
purple vowels .husky rhythms

of beaten laundry

far below under the slowness
of men in rice fields

but to write by any means
begins
first

by an idea such as
its fixedness

fixedness possible behind your sails
and your trailing colors
and also to turn pale

to assist you so upright   the
hands of your children
around the ankles

holding the rims of the basin of
detergent, basket of grains
teapot and jugs

under the shadow carcasses dangle
and stink. and I write the white
reiteration a new melody
far from the flies
and turbans

a box an orange
two stones

of lapis and amber

the other jewel inlaid
with red wood

whose name I ignore

while the book held open by the
ashtray and my eyeglass
case

on the left side of the page read
the customer notification
and horizon

read.   inside a music under
the keyboard
the game

of displacement the lieder
this memory equal to
driving forces

we will never come back
this is an audible idea
that for a long time
solicits my body

for I have the soul of a singer
you said it before me
I even loved you
for that

and then you you stopped
loving me for that but it's
not serious because
we will have

scattered there
yes from that
euph
oria

that euphoria in large hat
started up again today

by low water sand
heat and
evening

falling   .then
fallen

quality of the personnel sight of the river etc.
I wait for you you become the one
time flows outside

a strand of levity

quality of the personnel
sight of the river
from the rooms

one where I'll wait for you
where you'll come back

room where I view(ed) the years
herons, river smugglers
and the dust gone

with the wind the pirogues
and their fairies

quality of the personnel, sight of the river
from rooms and suites

in a park of flowering greenery
the grand hotel

reading comes from water .from your texts also on separation
man-servants are slowly working

and in the prayer that suspends all
we wait for mid-day

to cross the only bridge

advance of the return :if the screens are magical
I like to listen to the mystery of water and write
matte sound of my new necklaces

lines like minarets like
carts, forgetfulness
our moments all

visible same gift
same loss, it
would be
one day

the restored axis
of the world

a day restored
on the axis of
the world

a day on the axis
of the world
restored

a day a world
restored the
axis

a day of axis
not broken
will be

then yes th
e world lov
ed me

I'm hungry,   I miss you having lunch
with you I'm willing to reconnect

nets cast, waves on the water
voices that echo

since then somber silhouettes
and harmonica colors

we advance this way among kingdoms
of lonely beings where language
plays the world its reflection

in the lattice of
texts thrown

on swirls of swaying water
streams of sleep

shores of the lonely

who from their junk leave to marry
the features of this territory

that was given to them

.he then walked up to me
held out words inscribed
to effect commerce

here the child outside only knows how to beg

a coin for their hunger for their body
to welcome the masks

of the ancestors
he carries

another story today and
not the tireless infinite
one of loss

at the hour I write you

prose is the child today
in fact its face
tells

a story of pastries distributed by the militia
she pronounces: "a mountain of dead"

a film camera to armies
is difficult to imagine

really

wagon withdrawn from the museum. the dreaded arrives
two hours late. it resumes the place

the armistice .your name: Walter Benjamin

you your night of September 26-27 1940
at the border of all borders

Variation   6

notebook paper   ]   hard blue tint
oval of the world

rolls the shape of solstices
at the lapping-concert

of the stream   .your mouth
a canapé and on

the perfection of your features
here we are spread out

and if I write at your side this verse
the fig and its syllables

erased on behalf of a city by
a dream without support

a melody stoned   .steadily
without any of you

in which I
walk

walk a long time miserable the day
along the way and   this poem

at my heels it was
of a woman

well   .I notice the post office at the next artery
that leather merchant on the corner
of the pedestrian street

a bit further down   the newsstand
the historic square where
the dispossessed

are begging the servicemen
a hundred steps on white
tracings . my stroll

where I *rêve* on your arm
its a good thing because
the wish

flew by

it's you. I imitated you and in context
on strength of necessity   .clearing
the cleaning up of your room

week after week

sooner or later in the mesh of
stories the rail switches
fictions

you convinced me therefor I
weaved the wind burrowed

the score object of its form
the groan of the poem

this entity everywhere an hourglass
acts unraveled
usurping

in the dark urgency of the fixative
that affixes the expert
gesture

traces at the bottom of the basin
of this laundry bath
where soak

the remains of a   day
such as ours
that summer

summer this beautiful balance anise green and rose fuchsia
behind us the silence the clicking
of the electric meter

the forgetfulness on the beach one Sunday
where everything was possible

ahead of us she grabbed
leaving us to think it over

in the delivery room the
measure of your pulse
slight and mechanical

the graph of your small
quest I wait your
entrance

hand on the atomizer and your smile
here we are euphoric and calm

from any concept of equilibrium
a second secret exhale

distinguishes itself .outside
a newborn

.

how to believe in its unfamiliar
face   .therefore to decipher
her face and embrace
the embrace

to follow closely if that
is possible

if the waves pull out
toward us

you head at the vulva
me to the simple

to the simple like others to fists
you would be a reason for that
maybe even the reason

of the palpable poem that
comes from as far away
as you made

of instants you .waking
fixed and perfect
beautiful .re

invented

you .. legendary beauty
inverseuse versante
in the image

of a summit the summer
yes precisely this
season

that you carry
in a manner
of speaking

in front of us
have made
law

ignorant of what follows, noting right now
in the last page of the book:

to the one who came to be embodied

Points in Time:
Where the Body Was

Body Was by Isabelle Garron,
translated by Eléna Rivera

It takes a certain amount of courage in this age of the internet, where a plethora of words abound, to let the stillness and blank space speak. What I admire in Isabelle Garron's *Body Was* is its combination of lyricism and silence, the rhythm of the language and the way that she is able to let events, the overheard and experienced, move in and out of silence, into the body of the page. What remains of experience is stored in the body and what is written is already what was—the moment is gone. Time keeps moving. What was experienced is no longer the present. The experience is carried in the body. The body makes the text.

Body Was is a book-length poem that works on principles of improvisation, like that of Keith Jarrett, Glenn Gould and others, where the reader is drawn into a series of movements that rise and fall like waves. Lines become shorter, escape, without closure. Where the body "was" is already past. The past is where moments reside as fragments of our experience. A breath gives rise to emotions without trying to please. The death of a father is overheard and leaves its mark, as does walking up a mountain, or the birth of a child. These events resonate as moments of being, the place where the "body was."

The tone, rhythm and silences drive the poem forward. There is no beginning, no end, just the perpetual rhythm of life. In "Suites" and "Variations" words travel, renew and fall away, and what's left are glimpses, memories, experiences kept in the corporeal space. Garron works with the scattered fragments of biographical experiences, shattered under the impact of overlapping events while shedding light on the debris and enabling new understanding. She translates into language the intensely felt regret of the irreversibility of past experiences—the perpetual forward motion of reality closing in. In this book, Garron captures the subtleties of the mind's movements, a mode of composition in the footsteps of writers like Virginia Woolf, the William Carlos Williams of *Paterson*, and the French poets Stéphane Mallarmé, Pierre Reverdy (whom she was instrumental in having republished) and Anne Marie Albiach, among others.

I first came across Isabelle Garron's books when I read *Face devant contre*, which Sarah Riggs translated and introduced me to (published in Riggs' excellent translation by Litmus Press in 2007). I then translated "The Contemporary Step" a selection from *Qu'il Faille*, her second book (a piece made into a dance by choreographer Mani Mungai in France). I was drawn to translate *Body Was* by the intense pull of the language, its rhythm, its subtleties and absences. In translating this work, I wanted to achieve two things, first I wanted to be as accurate as possible and to that end worked closely with the author to make sure that I was as faithful to the original as I could be—faithful to its form as well as its content. The second thing I wanted was for this translation to convey the atmosphere of the original but in English, to convey my understanding of it and my appreciation for its images, sound, rhythm, form and language. The process of translation is about what emerges from the rubble of laying down words, side by side, above and below, on paper.

Translating for me, like writing a poem, is an act of discovery, a continual process of uncovering the layers of meaning, feeling, and pleasures of the poem. In a work like *Body Was*, where there are so many silences and unanswered questions, it is important not to try and elucidate the mysteries, but instead to enter them. The reader of the English must make their own journey and discoveries.

—Eléna Rivera

Acknowledgements

I am indebted to Isabelle Garron for her time answering my questions on all aspects of the translation; I am indeed fortunate for her friendship and collaboration.

Much gratitude to Sarah Riggs who first introduced me to Isabelle Garron's books, for her translation of Garron's first book *Face devant contre* (Litmus Press, 2002), and for·encouraging me to translate this book. I am equally grateful to Tamaas Poetry Translation Seminar for inviting me to participate in a week-long residency in Paris which allowed me to delve into the translation in earnest.

Thanks too to the Editions Flammarion for the permission to publish an English translation of this volume.

I am also grateful to Russell Switzer, E. Tracy Grinnell, Rachael Wilson, Mark Addison Smith, and everyone at Litmus Press who made this book possible.

About the Author

Isabelle Garron is a poet, critic, editor, and associate professor at the Institute Mines Telecom-Paristech. She is the author of *Bras vif* (Flammarion, 2018), *Corps fut* (Flammarion, 2011), *Qu'il Faille* (Flammarion, 2007), and *Face devant contre* (2002), which was translated into English by Sarah Riggs as *Face Before Against* (Litmus Press, 2008). With Yves di Manno, Garron co-edited an anthology of French poetry, *Un Nouveau monde: Poésies en France 1960–2010* (Flammarion, 2017).

About the Translator

Eléna Rivera is a poet and translator who was born in Mexico City and spent her formative years in Paris. She is the author most recently of *Epic Series* (Shearsman Books, 2020) and *Scaffolding* (Princeton University Press, 2017). She won the 2010 Robert Fagles prize for her translation of Bernard Noël's *I* (Graywolf Press, 2011) and is a recipient of a 2010 National Endowment for the Arts Literature Fellowship in Translation. Eléna has also received fellowships from the Djerassi Foundation, the Witter Bynner Poetry Translator Residency at the Santa Fe Art Institute, and the MacDowell Colony.